Building Character

Showing Respect

by Penelope S. Nelson

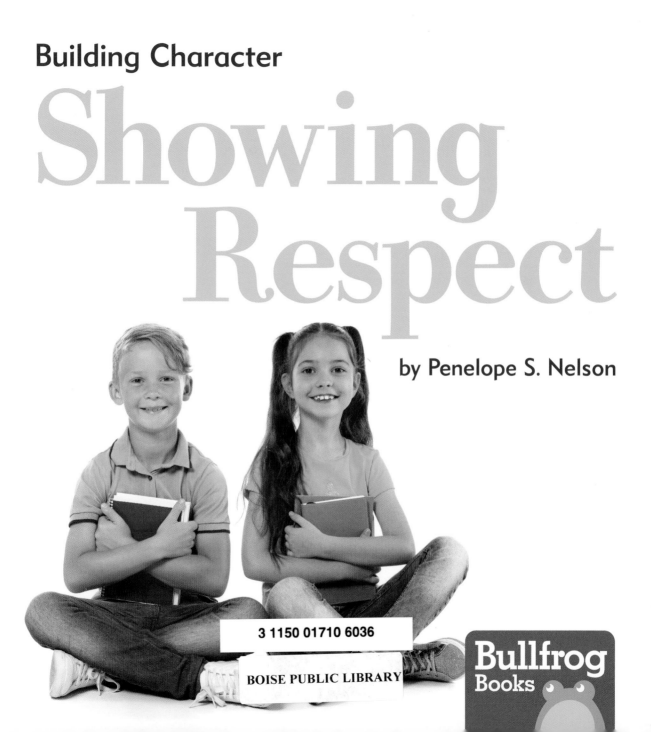

Bullfrog
Books

Ideas for Parents and Teachers

Bullfrog Books let children practice reading informational text at the earliest reading levels. Repetition, familiar words, and photo labels support early readers.

Before Reading
- Discuss the cover photo. What does it tell them?

- Look at the picture glossary together. Read and discuss the words.

Read the Book
- "Walk" through the book and look at the photos. Let the child ask questions. Point out the photo labels.

- Read the book to the child, or have him or her read independently.

After Reading
- Prompt the child to think more. Ask: Showing respect to others makes them feel good. Can you think of a time when someone showed you respect?

Bullfrog Books are published by Jump!
5357 Penn Avenue South
Minneapolis, MN 55419
www.jumplibrary.com

Library of Congress Cataloging-in-Publication Data

Names: Nelson, Penelope, 1994– author.
Title: Showing respect / by Penelope S. Nelson.
Description: Minneapolis, MN: Jump!, Inc., 2020.
Series: Building character | Includes index.
Audience: Age 5–8. | Audience: K to Grade 3.
Identifiers: LCCN 2018046170 (print)
LCCN 2018047622 (ebook)
ISBN 9781641287258 (ebook)
ISBN 9781641287234 (hardcover)
ISBN 9781641287241 (pbk.)
Subjects: LCSH: Respect—Juvenile literature.
Classification: LCC BJ1533.R4 (ebook)
LCC BJ1533.R4 N45 2020 (print) | DDC 179/.9—dc23
LC record available at https://lccn.loc.gov/2018046170

Editor: Jenna Trnka
Designer: Michelle Sonnek

Photo Credits: Bo Valentino/Shutterstock, cover; New Africa/Shutterstock, 1; naluwan/Shutterstock, 3; wavebreakmedia/Shutterstock, 4, 5, 6–7, 12–13, 23tl, 23tr, 23bm; Africa Studio/Shutterstock, 8–9, 19, 23tm; Darrin Henry/Shutterstock, 10–11; Es sarawuth/Shutterstock, 14; JGI/Jamie Grill/Blend Images/SuperStock, 15; TinnaPong/Shutterstock, 16–17; michaeljung/Shutterstock, 18, 23br; Tono Balaguer/Shutterstock, 20–21; HelenField/Shutterstock, 22 (drawing); Brooke Becker/Shutterstock, 22 (crayons); ratmaner/Shutterstock, 23bl; Chris Bourloton/Shutterstock, 24.

Printed in the United States of America at Corporate Graphics in North Mankato, Minnesota.

Table of Contents

Show You Care

Leah raises her hand.

She doesn't yell out.

Why?

She respects her teacher.

And her classmates.

We show respect.

Why?

To show we care.

We care about others' feelings.

Lou cares about
his family.

He does his chores.

He helps.

Min cares.

About who?

Her friends.

She shares.

Cool!

Max cares about
his belongings.

He takes care of them.

flag

We respect the flag. How?

We put our hands
on our hearts.

Cool!

Leo cares for the Earth.

How?

He keeps it clean.

He does not litter.

Mick cares
for himself.

He has good
self-esteem.

What else?

He cleans his body.

Nice!

We care.

How do you show it?

Places We Show Respect

We can show respect in many places. We can show it at home. At school. On the playground. Where do you show respect?

You will need:
- pieces of paper
- markers or crayons

Directions:
1. Fold each piece of paper in half. Unfold.
2. On one side of the crease, draw a picture of a place where you show respect.
3. On the other side of the paper, write ideas about how you can be respectful in each place.
4. Hang your drawings in a place where you will see them and remember to be respectful!

Being respectful at home

Picture Glossary

belongings
Possessions or things we own.

chores
Jobs, such as cleaning tasks, that need to be done regularly.

feelings
Thoughts or emotions.

litter
To leave garbage outside without throwing it away.

respects
Considers others and treats them kindly.

self-esteem
A feeling of personal pride and respect for yourself.

Index

To Learn More

FACT SURFER

Finding more information is as easy as 1, 2, 3.

❶ Go to www.factsurfer.com

❷ Enter "showingrespect" into the search box.

❸ Click the "Surf" button to see a list of websites.